TABL

REVIEWS

Reviews and feedback help improve this book and the author. If you enjoy this book, we would greatly appreciate it if you were able to take a few moments to share your opinion and post a review on Amazon.

FREE BONUS.
HYGGE GIFT IDEAS

Go to http://leadmagnet.epizy.com/
to download the guide for free

HYGGE

The Danish Secrets of Happiness:
How to Be Happy and Healthy in
Your Daily Life

Maya Thoresen

CHAPTER 1:

WHAT IS HYGGE?

According to the Oxford Dictionary, the word hygge (pronounced hue-guh) means "quality of coziness and comfortable conviviality that engenders a feeling of contentment or well-being." This is a Danish concept that is rooted in Danish and Norwegian culture. It is a way of life in this part of the world, and it might explain why those in this area of Europe experience a higher quality of living than other cultures. Hygge can be used to refer to all aspects of life in the form of a noun, verb, or adjective to describe something that falls under the hygge concept.

If you were to ask a Danish person what exactly hygge means, they would let you know it doesn't mean just one thing. There are numerous of elements that make up this way of living, and some of these you may already be doing without even knowing. There is no true English translation of the word, but the best words that come to mind when thinking about the hygge concept are cozy warm, content, comfortable, togetherness, and relaxation. These only skim the surface, though.

Hygge is particularly useful in the cold winter months, and that is how many believe the concept began. It made the winter season more bearable and comfortable for the Scandinavians.

It has, however, turned into a worldwide trend that has been gaining popularity in the last few years because of the simplicity of the concept. Often, Westerners complain about busy lives that never stop moving, and applying the hygge concepts to their daily lives can improve their overall lifestyle. Putting some of the hygge principles into practice can greatly improve the level of happiness a person feels as opposed to never taking the time to relax and just spend time with those they love.

CHAPTER 2:

HYGGE PRINCIPLES

As you have already learned, you can incorporate the Danish way of hygge into your life in many ways, all of which you will learn about throughout this book. The simplest way to begin is by learning the basic principles hygge teaches. These principles are the foundations of the lifestyle. Once you grasp these, you are well on your way to being able to implement them in your life, and, therefore, are on your way to happiness.

1. Mindfulness and the Senses

Mindfulness may be the hardest principle on the list, and yet, it is one of the most important if you are to find true happiness through this practice. Mindfulness means you are paying attention to the moment. You are fully engaged in whatever activity you are taking part of. This could be watching a movie, reading a book, or having a conversation over a cup of tea with a friend. This involves any moment in your life where you are absorbed at the moment, enjoying yourself and not worrying about the past or the future. Think of it as the saying "stop and smell the roses."

In the chaotic and fast-paced modern world, many of us forget to enjoy the moment because we are so busy thinking about that deadline we have to meet or the groceries we have to pick up for the week. Hygge encourages you to correct this problem. Let the aroma of a cup of coffee reach your nose before you take a sip. Enjoy the intricacies and colors of your loved one's eyes, and notice how soft your cotton sweater feels against your skin. Combining your attention without distractions with a full sensory experience helps you slow down the clock and enjoy your time. It can also help you create cherishable memories you can look back on later, even if it seems so simple at the time.

Mindfulness is a habit you must develop with time. You can't expect yourself to always be mindful; you have to work on it. One great way to achieve mindfulness is to simply stop what you are doing a minute or two each day and take in the world around you. When you are engrossed in a task and realize your mind is wandering, and pull it back to the present. Redirect your thoughts to the present moment until it becomes a habit for you to think in this way.

2. Gratitude and Being Positive

It may seem like common sense that looking at the positive side of things would make us feel happier, but that doesn't mean it is an easy practice. In fact, we may not even realize that we are not positive, at times.

The first rule of positivity in your daily life is feeling and expressing gratitude. When is the last time you told someone you appreciated them or thanked them for opening the door or helping you with the dishes? These are the little things we often forget, and it can make our days brighter because we are making someone else happy when we express gratitude. When we feel grateful for something we are also feeding on the positive flow of energy from the person, we have thanked. A simple show of thanks can go a long way, especially if someone has had a horrible day.

14

The rest of positivity is about finding that bright spot in the darkness. This world is a chaotic one that can sometimes lead to heartache. There is no denying that, but you can often find something good in your life, even in the worst circumstances.

Think and act positively in all you do. Choose to talk about the good things instead of voicing complaints, and look for sources of good news instead of overwhelming yourself and feeling down about all the tragedies that are happening around the world. It is important to be informed, but not to the point to feel depressed due to dark headlines.

3. Nature

If you know anything about the Nords and their traditions, you saw this one coming. Being active in nature is considered not only calming but inspiring. Nature is what we come from. Even if our buildings and conveniences make our lives easier, there is still a part within each of us that calls out to the wild. This is a great way to practice using all your senses, as well. Smelling flowers, feeling the cold chill of the wind on your cheek and seeing the bright colors of spring are enough to make anyone appreciate and love the world around them.

It is important to incorporate nature into your life. Go on hikes. Go to the beach. Bring potted plants into your home décor. Do everything that you can to get outside, and bring your family along to enjoy time together.

4. Ease and Comfort

This is something that can easily be expressed through what you wear and how things are done in your home. One of the words used to describe the word of hygge is cozy, and that is what you are trying to achieve. Surround yourself with things that bring you comfort and warmth.

Using soft, comfortable pillows rather than flashy, impractical ones; spending the day in a loose pair of those beloved sweatpants, and choose to go makeup-free for the day are examples of ways you can practice this principle in your life. Comfort and ease go hand-in-hand.

Choose to abandon the discomforts of life if you can. Of course, you can't always avoid discomfort. It is an inevitable part of life. But sometimes you endure uncomfortable things because you choose to. You don't have to. If you have a pair of shoes that look nice but feel horrible, donate them or throw them out. You don't need to sacrifice comfort for temporary beauty. If there is someone around you who makes you uncomfortable or gives off a negative presence, don't feel as if you have to keep them in your life. If talking it over doesn't work, it's better to free yourself from that negativity and bad influence and focus on the people that bring happiness and comfort to your life. You should evaluate things that you don't like or want to do and cut them out if you can.

Making life easier does *not* make you lazy. It makes you smart. If you find a way to streamline work or automate your technology, then do so. You are busy and tired enough—why add stress to your life by doing things the hard way? Remember, comfort and ease are the important factors in your new lifestyle.

5. Togetherness

The Danish believe in spending quality time with one another. Friends and loved ones should take up a good portion of your time, even if it feels hard to make time in your busy schedule. Don't you feel better after a cup of coffee with your best friend or a Netflix night with your spouse? There is a reason for that. We are all connected, and we are all meant to complement one another. You cannot have true happiness

16

without taking advantage of that.

One of the major principles of this time spent with those you care for, though, relates back to mindfulness. It means giving your full attention to the people that you are with. Cell phones and other distractions that keep you distant and partially at the moment are put to the side in favor of conversation and physical closeness. Stop letting insignificant distractions get in the way of truly being there with your loved ones.

Remember that none of us live forever. So, appreciate the people you love while they are still here. Although this is a morbid thought to have, focus on how you can enjoy your time with them as long as they are still here, not the limitations of time. Be mindful and stay in the moment with them, avoiding both internal and external distractions.

Plenty of us is taught to keep our problems to ourselves. We don't want to burden other people with the things that bother or distress us. We feel like inconveniences when we are upset or have a problem. But hygge encourages you to connect with the people you care for. Part of forging that connection is reaching out to your family when you need help. Talk to them and share what is bothering you. Form stronger bonds with them by letting them into your life, your mind, and your heart. You can't deal with life alone, and you will enjoy and appreciate having the support of them by your side.

6. Pleasure

Hygge is all about enjoying the simple pleasures of life. Can you honestly say that you do that? You may take a vacation or two every year and make time for a fancy date night once a month, but this principle is actually something even simpler than that. Hygge pleasure is about slowing down and enjoying the small things that you don't have to look far for. This could be your favorite dessert, a walk along the beach with the feeling of sand in your toes, or the laughter of your children as you tickle them. We need to learn to find these moments and make them happen. Pleasure with a hygge lifestyle is about the experience around us instead of lavish gifts and large events at an expense.

There are countless pleasurable moments around you all the time. Majority of us fail to pay attention to them. One of life's little secrets is that the wealth and pleasure you work hard for and wait for is usually disappointing. You could slave away for a lavish vacation only to have things go wrong, not enjoying the time off. You save up for months to buy that product you want, only to find that it doesn't work as well as you wanted. You work tirelessly at your job to increase your wealth, only to find that years have passed and you don't have as much time to enjoy the fruits of your labor. When you put pleasure on a pedestal and delay it and strive for it, it will evade you. It will never fail to disappoint. When you accept pleasure as something that surrounds you and something that you create with your attitude, then you will find that pleasure is much more abundant and available than you think.

Pleasure does not require time, money, or other people. It requires attitude. You must be open to pleasure; you must accept it without trying to change it or control it. You must look for it in the world around you and be grateful for it when you find it. The pleasure lies in the little moments. Embrace those moments. You will get into the habit of finding them more and more throughout your day when you start to adopt the hygge attitude and lifestyle.

Of course, you don't have to lie back and wait for pleasure to come to you. You can deliberately create a more pleasant atmosphere and the situation in your life. That is a large part of what this book is about. Hygge is something that comes naturally, but you can do many things to increase it and bring it about in your life. If something brings you pleasure, why not add it to your life and boost your mood as a result?

8. Minimalism and Quiet

Part of hygge is the belief that minimalism will bring you peace and happiness. This goes for every facet of life, but especially for your home décor. Having the bare minimum that you need in furniture with a simple layout and including a quiet corner to have some time alone to read or meditate can make you feel less cluttered.

Excess amounts of stuff stress you out and bog down your energy. You have too many things to worry about and organize and clean. There is no need for so much stuff. Having a more minimal lifestyle allows you to breathe, both literally and metaphorically.

You might consider Swedish death cleaning. This type of cleaning is a decluttering method where you ask yourself, "What do I really need in my life?" It encourages you to cut out excess things that you don't need. Consider how your loved ones will have to clean out your house when you pass away. The more excessive junk you have, the more stress they will have to deal with. You can minimize that potential stress by getting rid of the things you can live without. Let yourself be freer by cutting out clutter.

If you can't let go of something for some sentimental reason, then keep it but find clever ways to store things. Or invest in a storage unit. Give it time. After a while of not living with it and not seeing it, do you still want it? Or can you safely get rid of it, knowing you won't miss it?

Another tip is to hang your clothes backward. When you wear clothes and put them away again, hang them the right way. At the end of the year, if there are any clothes left that are still facing the wrong way, you know that you never wore them. You can probably get rid of them without regret.

Consider donating things instead of throwing them away. One man's trash is another man's treasure. You might just make someone's day by giving him or her something for free or at an affordable price. The act of being kind to others can give you a warm sense of pleasure, which is all part of hygge.

CHAPTER 3:

HYGGE AT HOME

Much of the hygge tradition is practiced within the home, so it stands to reason that you would need to change your home, at least a little, to reflect your new lifestyle. When at home, your happiness should be centered around it as a place to relax and be yourself with your friends and family. Your home is a precious sanctuary where you can unwind and be your authentic self. All of your worries and stresses need to be left at the door. Doesn't that sound like a better life than you are living now?

HYGGE DÉCOR

Hygge décor is simple in more ways than one. It is easy to incorporate into any home, and the décor itself is aesthetically pleasing. Minimalism and simplicity are what your home should feel like to you. Instead of creating a chaotic home that bogs you down with mess and induces stress with constant organizing and cleaning, try to simplify things. Often the most beautiful homes are designed by simplicity. Ever noticed homes that are stuffed with things and clashing décor aren't pleasing to the eye?

However, your home is a place that should bring you pleasure. Therefore, you want it to look a way that appeals to you. You want to fill it with things you enjoy looking at. You want to add items that give your home that special unique quality that says *you*.

Your home décor should also be useful and functional. A large glass figurine that is easy to break in a home with a lot of activity, or a coffee table that is expensive you are afraid to set anything on it, is not practical. Useless décor serves to be monetarily wasteful, and you could use that space for things you actually need and utilize. Let's consider an example. If you love playing pool but find that you don't have room for a pool table because of your fancy coffee table, ask yourself, "Do I ever use that coffee table?" Replace the coffee table with the pool table and rearrange your furniture. Or consider a sofa set with many pieces in your home that makes it difficult to navigate the living room. Why not get rid of the couches you don't use and replace them with things like a bookshelf or a TV that you actually use?

Go for décor that is simple and functional, preferably in light or warm colors. Pastels or warm colors are more cheerful than dark, depressing colors. Be sure everything that is meant for comfort is comfortable and make use of texture. You can incorporate texture with pillows, blankets, rugs, and other accessories that make you feel great when you feel them between your fingers. Replace stiff, uncomfortable things that are for a show with items that feel good.

Much of the best décor can be found in places such as Etsy, where many crafty individuals find it a passion for creating hygge items and accessories. Handmade items are often more comfortable, have a personal flair to them, and are pleasing to look at. Plus, they add character to your home.

When it comes to making space in your home, you can go to the Container Store or order cute storage bins and shelves online. Store your stuff out of the way and keep it organized neatly. You can ensure that your storage is both attractive and functional. Having clutter everywhere to trip over is not functional nor attractive. It is far better to put things in proper places. It will make your home inviting and easier to clean.

HYGGE AND ANIMALS

Another hygge element in existence is a pet. Pets can offer comfort and are calming, and adorable to have around. You can find that pets relieve stress and bring joy to your life. Pick a pet that suits your lifestyle without difficulty, while also getting joy from it. A snake may not be the best option if you are afraid of reptiles or do not know how to care for one, for instance. A dog may not be ideal if you don't have time and will worry about it too much while you are at work.

CREATING A HYGGE ATMOSPHERE

As you know, hygge is all about how it makes you feel, so even if you have only some simple and comfortable furniture, this is a great start. Fill every room with something that makes you feel cozy. Try Egyptian cotton sheets on your bed, cashmere clothes for relaxing on the sofa, and scents in your bathroom that soothe and heal you such as lavender. If you surround yourself with little things that make you feel good, you will soon find you are a much happier and healthier person on the inside.

Other items such as a drawing your child made at school, a sentimental treasure from your childhood, or stuffed animals are all things that you can add to each room to bring you that warm fuzzy feeling of being home. Sometimes, it is okay to sacrifice perfection and beauty for comfort. If you have something that doesn't quite match your home's theme, but still makes you happy, then put it up! You will be creating a conversation piece while lightening your mood when you are home.

Creating a hygge lifestyle and atmosphere doesn't require you to go out and spend a fortune on new décor, especially if you don't have the budget for it. This will only increase your stress and defies the basic concept of hygge. Instead, use what you have. Or buy small, inexpensive things. If you can, splurge on a few items that you absolutely love to get high-quality pieces that bring you comfort and joy. That said, don't go on a huge shopping spree and spend money you don't have.

If your home makes you happy as it currently is, and if it is full of joy and cheer, then perhaps you don't need to change much or even anything at all—it is clearly perfect for your needs. But if your home depresses you, stresses you out, or embarrasses you in some way, it may be time for some changes. Your home environment impacts your mood significantly, so make it something you can enjoy living in. You will notice an improvement in your life when you change your home to reflect who you truly are and what you like.

THE IMPORTANCE OF CANDLES

Imagine a time before there was electricity when heat and light came from fires and candles. Danish winters were bitter cold, and hygge was as much of a necessity as it was something beautiful to hold onto. Wrapping up in blankets and gathering around the fire or using candles to illuminate a room to tell stories or enjoy a delicious meal doesn't have to be a thing of the past. The warm glow of a candle, as well as the soothing scents many come in, can work wonders on your mood. You can enjoy this old-time practice and use candles to enhance your home for little money.

In hygge homes, you will find many candles lit year-round. Using candles is often the first step in creating a new hygge way of living as it is the most iconic piece of the puzzle.

You can go with simple tea lights or find a beautiful candle with a scent that makes you feel relaxed. Find pretty candle holders that play with the light in attractive ways. You can also utilize lamps and natural salt lamps to create a warm, romantic ambiance. The options are endless—it's up to you to find out what you like for your home!

HYGGE IN YOUR PERSONAL SPACE

Hygge is all about creating a personal space where you can leave your cares behind and simply enjoy the act of existing. Part of the hygge lifestyle is creating a personal space where you can become mindful and leave your stress, worry, and pain at the door. Your personal space does not have to be the whole house, especially if you share your house with other people. It can simply be a room or even a corner in a room. It is a small, comfortable space where you can be your authentic self. You can go there to recharge after a long day and engage in your hobbies.

Make your personal space uniquely yours. Decorate it however you want. Common features are pleasing aromas, comfortable furniture, and cushy pillows, and lights that make you feel warm and at peace.

Remember that your personal space is all yours. You can expect to be left alone here. Tell others that if you are in your personal space, they should leave you be. Only invite in the people that bring you joy and make you feel good. Toxic and annoying people should stay at the door! Because you are using this space for relaxing, try to remove electronics and communication devices from the area. Let this space cradle you and melt away your worries when you are in it. You don't need to be dinged by work when you are in your space.

Remember to use your personal space for what you enjoy doing. A personal space could be a craft room or a yoga studio. It could be a studio where you paint or an office where you write. If you love cooking, it could be your well-stocked kitchen where you create many culinary delights. It could be your man cave, where you watch football and enjoy a beer after work. It could simply be your half of the bed, where you meditate and write in your journal before bed. Just make sure that this space is functional for what you choose to do it. No one can tell you what to do in your personal space because it is yours.

CHAPTER 4:

HYGGE AT WORK

Hygge may seem to have nothing to do with business or work. After all, the very idea of work is often not relaxing or cozy. It recalls the image of agonizingly long days and lots of stress, which is the common work environment for most Americans and Europeans. Longer work hours, leading to less of a work-life balance is a problem, especially in American culture. Working hard is an admirable quality in American workers, often to the point where Americans get sick from stress and lack of breaks. Family leave is disappearing, and many feel pressured to not take any of their vacation time.

It does not have to be this way, though. You may not be able to control every aspect of your job or career, but you can start making small changes here and there to ease the burden, especially if you're looking to head in the direction of freedom, like by being a solopreneur. Make your workplace as hygge as possible to reduce stress and displeasure.

Adjust your attitude about work. Work is not life. You work to live; you should not live to work. Work is not the sole priority, so set limits on how much you work and when work can contact you. This is not always possible in some fields. If you are on call, try to make the best of your free time to do hobbies or be with your family. Conserve your time as best you can in your line of work.

Not everyone can do what they love. But if you can, then do it without fear or doubt. Maybe it is the time that you open your dream restaurant or quit your job to try traveling the world and making money blogging. Sometimes you may need to sacrifice money for happiness. Adjust your attitude to value happiness over money, and take a pay cut to do what you love. When you die, the amount of money you made will not matter to you half as much as how happy you were.

Evaluate your budget to determine what you can give up and how much money you can safely lose if you need to change your career. Take some vacation time when you can afford it. Maybe reduce your hours or even take a new job that you enjoy. It is more important to have a life you enjoy than a lot of expensive material possessions. Hygge encourages you to value moments and experiences over meaningless possessions and money.

Some people are lucky enough to do what they love. The only problem with this is that it is easy for these people to forget about other important elements of life as they become addicted to their jobs. If you are such a person, remember that there is more to life than your job. As exciting as your job is, you need to do other things you love, too, such as spend time with your family or exercise outside. Never devote everything you have to your job because your job is only a fraction of what your life is about.

MAKE YOUR SURROUNDINGS MORE HYGGE

By now, you know very well that the décor and colors used in a room can greatly affect the mood and productivity of a person. Danish offices look different than those in other countries. This is because the Danish understand the work environment can influence how you work and how you feel about the work.

Whether you are working at a desk, in an office, or at home, make sure your workspace is clean and uncluttered. Being organized can stop the day from being too hectic and can make you feel better all around. Imagine how much time you will save if you are not busy looking for things in a huge mess. Imagine how much better you will feel if you walk into a clear space where you can breathe and not worry about stepping on something or having something fall on you.

If you have any say in the décor and color around you, choose light colors or white with a pattern. This is the ideal décor that is not distracting and will not negatively affect mood or performance. You don't need tons of pictures or distracting knick-knacks on your walls or desk. However, you can really enhance your mood at work by having a few things that bring you joy, such as a nice note from a boss or customer, or a cute photo of your kids.

Some people find benefit from a vision board, where they attach pictures of their goals and cherished things. You can use a vision board to help you visualize your goals and feel inspired to achieve those goals. Use it as a means for productivity and mood enhancement.

Use a comforting scent. If you have a stressful job, try a lavender diffuser to bring relaxation into your atmosphere. If you need energy, try a more energizing scent like citrus or rosemary. If you need comfort in an emotionally challenging job, find a scent that reminds you of good times and use a Glade plug-in or scented candle to bring into your workspace. For just a few bucks, you can get a wax warmer that will diffuse scent throughout your workspace.

Comfort is key. You can't expect to work well if your

environment is unpleasant and uncomfortable. Ergonomic keypads, mice, chairs, and desks can add so much comfort to your workplace. You can also add a cushion or neck pillow to make your chair more comfortable. If you can't decorate your workspace as you please, then just add little things, like a colorful tissue box or a jar of candy. Be sure to wear comfortable shoes and clothes. Even in a formal setting, you don't have to wear business clothes that make you want to faint. If you walk during your commute to work, you can wear comfortable shoes such as tennis shoes or sandals and just carry your work shoes in your bag to change into at the office. Make sure your clothes match the current weather so that you can maintain good body temperature and don't wear anything so tight that it digs into your skin as you work. If you have to wear a uniform, make sure it fits and loosen it up by undoing a button or taking off your belt during your downtime.

ATTITUDE

The way you look at situations can greatly change how you feel about them, and sometimes it can even change the outcome. Hygge at work is all about your attitude and the way you carry yourself.

First of all, remove the urgency. Even if you have an urgent deadline or are in the business of saving lives, you can reduce stress by removing the idea that your job is life or death. Your job very well may be life or death, but don't focus on that. Instead, focus on the tasks at hand. Don't think, "I have to do this by midnight, or it is over for me!" Think, "I have this many steps to complete before I reach my deadline at midnight. So this is how I will divvy up the tasks over the remaining hours."

Approach things from a problem-solving angle. Don't focus

30

on what might happen if you fail, or what you stand to lose. This reduces your stress and makes work more pleasurable. When your mind wanders, use mindfulness to bring it back into focus.

Confidence is also key to reducing your stress and improving your mood. You don't feel that great when you are busy criticizing yourself or feeling inadequate, do you? Believe in yourself. Let yourself take calculated risks that will grow your business or your team's performance. Try innovative things. If you fail, learn from that experience instead of beating yourself up over it.

When you are confident in your abilities, you can look beyond yourself and seek out others who are good at what they do. Cooperation is what makes businesses run well. When you are confident, you don't become egotistical and jealous of others. Rather, you are open to appreciating and working with others. You let your ego down and become open to others. That's a great way to be at work. Work will be easier when you strive to work with others and make valuable connections, without letting jealousy and ego get in the way. Your confidence will also make you more attractive to others, so they will want to talk to you and work with you.

Reach out to your co-workers and have fun with them. Work hard to collaborate with others. If you prefer to work alone, at least make water cooler chitchat to connect with others in your workplace. The day will go by faster, and you will rest easier knowing that you have co-workers who will help you out when you need it.

Finally, keep the attitude that your work is only part of your life. Place value on other things, like hobbies and family. You will learn more about this in the following section.

WORK-LIFE BALANCE

Hygge encourages you to live your life moment by moment. It tells you to be with your family and friends. That can be quite difficult when you are stuck at work all the time. You must strike a balance between work and the rest of your life. Devote some time to work, but use good time management to get everything done. Then set boundaries and don't work when you don't have to. Take some time for yourself and your loved ones where work may not intrude.

Work-life balance calls for you to find time for things other than work. This means that you should not feel guilty or afraid of taking a vacation. This means that you don't answer work emails when you are at home with your family. This means that when you are out at dinner, you don't answer your phone when it rings. Have automatic vacation responses set up on your email that tells people when you will get back to them. As tempting as it is to respond right then and there, get back to them when you say you will, not during your time off. Most people are accepting and understanding when you set these boundaries. Without these boundaries, your workaholic nature will become the standard that people expect from you.

If your job does not allow you to have a work-life balance, then consider switching jobs or even careers. It may take some time to move into a new position, but you should work for it. You need a job that does not treat you like a machine.

CHAPTER 5:

HYGGE AND RELATIONSHIPS

Wouldn't it be nice if some of the stress and drama could be removed from your relationships? It may seem impossible to think that simply changing your lifestyle a little could make you happier in all of your relationships. People spend years in therapy to try and get it right and sometimes still fail. Well, hygge cannot guarantee compatibility, but it can help you be happier in your dealings with your spouses, parents, and children if everyone can compromise and make a few adjustments.

FINANCIAL SOUNDNESS

How many fights have you had involving money? Danish marriages, excluding the royal family perhaps, are much different from many other marriages around the world.

Firstly, the average age of men and women getting married is above 30 for both. This means that many individuals are already financially settled before they bring another person into the mix. No matter what age you are when you get married, strive to be financially sound before you make that jump. If you are already married, then take some time to focus on outlining and achieving your financial goals. You should work hard together to remove the financial strife that causes problems in your marriage.

Many Danish people also do not have the kind of lavish

weddings that so many other women feel pressured to have. Many Western women are looking to outdo every other female with their weddings, and a high price tag often means years of credit card debt. That may not be the best way to start out a new family, even if the wedding is a beautiful moment. Also, the wedding should be about the couple, not pleasing and impress everyone else. A simpler wedding is sometimes better. Consider minimizing stress and focusing on enjoying your partner instead of having an enormous fancy wedding.

Throughout the marriage, as well, sound decisions are made by the Danish to ensure savings and living only within their means. It doesn't take a genius to realize that removing those fights over bills you don't know how to pay could bring you and your partner much closer together. Create a budget together and stick to it. If you don't need something or can't afford it, then don't buy it. Focus more on enjoying little moments together than squandering money on what you don't really need.

NO DRAMA

The drama has become a part of American culture somehow, and everyone seems to find a way to create it or place themselves inside of it, whether intentional or not. Then they wonder why divorce rates are so high and why they are so unhappy. The drama has no place in a healthy relationship, and picking your battles is important. Being right isn't always going to feel good when it means going to bed alone.

Of course, you will fight, but try to fight fair. Don't reduce it to name-calling and drudging up past wrongs. Fight with a purpose, and do not go to bed angry. Try to reach a resolution rather than hurting each other. You have heard it a million times, but fighting fair really is key, and in all relationships, not just romantic ones.

34

ENJOYING EACH OTHER

This may go without saying, but the way people spend time together today is not the way they used to or the way that is conducive to the best relationship possible. When you are with someone you love, you should be at the moment. Clear your hands of electronics and your thoughts on stresses and tasks at work and at home. Whether you are taking a walk, watching a movie, or having a candlelit dinner together, you and your loved one should take the time to pay close attention to each other. This will bring you closer in ways you did not think was possible.

CREATING ROMANTIC MOMENTS

In a romantic relationship, you want to create romantic moments. These romantic moments don't entail expensive dinners at fancy five-star restaurants or island vacations that break your bank for years to come. They don't involve presents of diamonds or hundred-dollar rose bouquets. Sure, those things are romantic, and you can practice them with your partner whenever you can, but you can create romance even when you are broke or tired after work. All you have to do is be thoughtful and think of what your partner may want.

Offer your partner a foot rub or a bubble bath after a long day at work. Surprise him or her with his or her favorite dinner. Suggest an evening walk. Pick some flowers and present your partner with a handmade bouquet. These little things show that you care. When you make an effort, your partner will notice and reciprocate. Thus, your relationship will get stronger and better.

Also, consider having more deep conversations with your partner. Conversation bonds you two closer. It helps you get to know each other. Your partner will feel more loved and appreciated if you take some time to talk to him or her. Simply taking the time to ask about his or her day and thank him or her for being in your life can make a world of difference. Some married couples careening toward divorce have been able to save their marriages simply by saying thank you more often and asking each other about their days.

CHAPTER 6:

HYGGE AS A PARENT

The parent-child relationship is often overlooked when it comes to improving the way you feel with other people, but it is easily the most important relationship you will ever have. Your relationship with your children sets up a model for their future relationships. It is important to cultivate love, trust, and independence. Hygge can be a huge help in doing this, and Danish parenting may give you relief if you are struggling with how things are going with your children. Here are some hygge tips on parenting that might help turn a chaotic home into a more loving and comfortable one:

- Redirecting as the first line of discipline instead of going straight to spanking or timeout may help the child better, especially later in life. Many acts of misbehavior have to do with emotions that a child just does not know how to express yet. Redirect the child on how to express themselves properly, and the behavior will change. Ask him or her, "What are you feeling right now? Is there another way you can show what you are feeling instead of [insert bad behavior]?"

- Playing is growing. There is a reason the Montessori Method is beginning to catch on in schools. The play is considered an essential part of learning and development for children. Play with them often, and let them use their imagination. This will foster excellent critical thinking skills in young adulthood.

- Have children help with chores as soon as they are physically able. Not only will chores get done quicker, meaning more time for fun together, but children will also feel more self-worth knowing that they can help an adult with something.
- Have uninterrupted time together where everyone enjoys doing things as a family. Turn off electronics and be with your kids wholeheartedly. Have meaningful conversations with them and get to know them as an individual, as hard as it may be to consider them anything but your baby. Let them express themselves. Make sure there is something in it for everyone. No one is excluded, and all of you are in the moment with each other. As always, turn those phones off.

HYGGE FAMILY MOMENTS

It is easy to create family moments that you can cherish for years to come. Make memories together by doing little things. From fishing trips to day excursions to local museums, use the resources available to you to create little moments together. You don't have to spend a lot of money to enjoy family moments.

One of the most common key family moments is dinnertime. Turn off all phones and the TV. Most people today have busy schedules they hardly have time to sit down and eat, but make a conscious effort to get all family members at the dinner table every evening. Sit down and eat together, even if it isn't Thanksgiving. Talk about each other's days. This will create a bond your family, making you closer as a unit. If you have a family member who absolutely cannot eat with you because of work or school, coordinate your schedules and set aside a few hours to spend time together. Just trying to spend time together will mean a lot to your family and encourage them to make time for you.

CHAPTER 7:

HYGGE IN THE SEASONS AND HOLIDAYS

CHRISTMAS

Christmas is one of the most hygge holidays because it is naturally cozy. Invite Christmas into your home by setting up for the holidays ahead of time. Focus more on having family gatherings with hot cocoa, singing carols, and making cookies together, than on buying the most expensive presents for each other and decorating your house the most lavishly out of your neighbors. Remember what Christmas is about: love, cheer, and coziness.

OTHER HOLIDAYS

While Christmas is possibly the most hygge holiday of its own accord, you can make every holiday hygge by really getting into the holiday spirit. Go all out with candy for trick-or-treaters and have fun on Halloween, and enjoy great food and express gratitude for your many blessings on Thanksgiving. Give your kids candy on Easter. Go to local events and spend time with family and friends. These things entail embracing the holidays and enjoying the moment. This is hygge in a nutshell.

Some people feel disgruntled or annoyed when the holidays roll around. Why not enjoy yourself? The holidays don't have to be stressful or commercial, just because the media and others around you make them so. Rather, the holidays are an excuse to take a break from work and enjoy yourself and eat a lot of good food.

Forget about your diet. Forget about being the best. Let go of work concerns. Just let the holiday spirit overtake you and make it a special time for yourself and your loved ones.

SPRING

Spring is a fun time when the earth begins to wake up from winter. The cold lingers, but the days are pleasant. Take advantage of the energy of spring by doing some spring cleaning and airing out your house. Start to go outside and show your kids the magic of nature by pointing out bird nests and budding flowers.

SUMMER

Summer is a fun time when you can enjoy yourself outside. Make the most of summer by getting in touch with nature. Plan a lot of outdoor excursions and hikes. Plant a garden and try to grow some of your own fruits and vegetables. If you have kids, they will love the experience of growing food, too. Take advantage of the precious summer months and the fact that school is out to spend time with your family. Embrace the short time that summer allows for outdoor barbecues, firecrackers, and sports like volleyball, swimming, or softball.

AUTUMN

Autumn is a cooling down time when you can enjoy the transition from summer to winter. Use this period to prepare your house for the coming winter and fill it with candles and warm blankets. Make warm soups and teas. Harvest your garden and enjoy the fruits of your labor. If you have a lot of trees in your yard, rake the leaves and proceed to play in the piles with your pet or your kids, or even your romantic partner, for some silly fun. Go for hikes in the brisk autumn air and observe the migrating birds. These activities allow you to embrace the essence of fall.

WINTER

Danish winters are cold and dark and seem to last forever. Do the Danish let this get them down? No, they make the best of winters by inviting warmth, coziness, and cheer into their homes. Don't let snow and darkness get you down, but rather, make a game of playing in the snow and use winter as an excuse to make a lot of warm, delicious food. Bring out your comfy sweaters and sweatpants and slippers. While shoveling snow and salting the driveway, sing songs to keep you warm and have your kids help.

CHAPTER 8:

FOOD AND DRINKS

Did you know that the concept of hygge comes with its own diet? Well, it's not exactly the kind of diet you are thinking of. It is not guaranteed to help you lose weight or is even something that should be in play with every single meal, but when you are practicing the happy Danish lifestyle and get the full experience to make it perfect and bring it all together, foods and drinks can do this for you if you know what to make. With an emphasis on comfort food, great smells, and warmth, how could you not want to give it a try?

SCANDI COMFORT FOODS

If you never had Scandinavian comfort food, you are truly missing out. There is something special about every aspect of this food, and there is nothing that says hygge more than sitting down to slowly enjoy a delicious, homemade meal with friends and family. That is truly the point of this comfort; you eat in comfort. There is no rush. There is a steady conversation throughout the meal that you savor, just as a meal is meant to be. Can you incorporate a meal like this once a week? If you would like to try, there are many hygge recipe books out there as the concept is gaining popularity around the world. Many cultures want to delve into the hygge lifestyle to find true happiness. In a hygge cookbook, you might find comfort food recipes involving ingredients such as:

- Duck
- Potatoes
- Rye Bread
- Quinoa Salad
- Apples

WARM DRINKS

Hygge drinks are traditionally meant for those cold winter nights spent curled up in front of a fire. The aromas are soothing, making you think of your childhood, the holidays, and pure warmth, and so is the temperature of the drink itself. It shouldn't be hard to think of something warm you like to drink, but just in case, here are some of the best suggestions:

- Apple Cider
- Coffee
- Herbal or Green Tea
- Hot Chocolate

A HYGGE RECIPE FOR EVERY MEAL

If you have never cooked any Scandinavian comfort food before, or anything even close, you might be wondering what to try. Obviously, baking is a huge part of the Scandinavian cuisine, but you can't live exclusively on bread and cookies, as much as you might like to. So, we have prepared one suggestion for each meal to get you started. That is three days you can pick from to try a new comforting meal with your whole family. The best part is that many of the recipes for hygge meals can be prepared safely as a family, allowing you to spend even more time with your loved ones. This is a precious commodity if work and school always seem to get in the way of quality time.

For breakfast, try an apple turnover or similar pastry. Many Europeans have their sweet treats in the morning to get them going for the day, and it has been working for them for many years. Why not try your hand at it and see how you feel?

For lunch, nothing says Danish better than a warm and hearty soup. There are many varieties to choose from that are all delicious. However, pumpkin soup is by far the general favorite. You can dress it up any way you want and drink it right out of a large mug.

For dinner, why not try something savory? Roasted pork is a common staple at the dinner table in Denmark. Pair it with a baked potato for an indulgent meal that does not involve anything fried or pre-made. This is the exact kind of meal you can savor at the table with your loved ones.

There are many places you can find hygge recipes online. Here are the three best below:

- http://www.organicauthority.com/discovering-danish-food-with-9-recipes-to-make-you-feel-the-hygge/
- http://www.self.com/gallery/13-healthy-hygge-foods-for-the-coziest-day-ever
- https://www.brit.co/hygge-foods-recipes/

CHAPTER 9:

HYGGE CLOTHES

Hygge does not place emphasis on appearances. Rather, it emphasizes how you feel. It is better to be lounging on the couch in sweats enjoying yourself than looking like a beauty king or queen. While looking good has its benefits, it is not the most important thing in life. You will enjoy life more if you relax.

Danish clothes are often simple and functional. They don't look bad, but they don't sacrifice quality for appearance. Wearing simple, clean, quality clothes is essential to your comfort. Clothes with pockets are useful to can carry things in. You want clothes that don't restrict your body or make you hold a ridiculous posture all day long.

Go for a good fit, not a tight fit. Also, go for materials that feel good to you. Cotton is light and breathable during summer. Warm wool and wool blends are nice during winter. You can get the most out of sweat-wicking polyester when you are engaged in strenuous tasks or sports that make you sweat.

Shoes should also be comfortable. Why wear skyscraper heels when you have to walk, or tight shoes that hurt your toes and give you blisters? Instead, wear practical shoes that fit you well. Sometimes you must sacrifice beauty for comfort—otherwise, your day could often be disrupted by your aching feet. An oozing blister is not worth the compliments you'll receive. It's better to buy shoes that fit and able to walk around in with ease.

CHAPTER 10:

HYGGE OUTSIDE OF THE HOME

Deciding to live the hygge lifestyle doesn't mean making your home your only place of comfort and staying there all the time. You can experience this Danish way of happiness anywhere you go. In fact, Danish vacations and family activities fall right into many of the principles you learned earlier in the book such as ease, coziness, and togetherness. Picnics, short trips, and playing games are all a part of the Danish culture, as well. Look at the list below for some ideas on how to incorporate hygge in all aspects of your life including activities outside the home.

15 IDEAS FOR HYGGE ACTIVITIES

1. Cook a special meal together as a family.
2. Play a board game or do a puzzle together.
3. Have a picnic in a quiet and serene place.
4. Take a family bike ride through the country or a beautiful trail.
5. Take a road trip and stop at one spot for each family member.
6. Take a weekend camping trip.
7. Go somewhere where it snows and play in the snow together.
8. Have hot chocolate by a fire and watch a family movie.

9. Go fishing together.
10. Read a classic book as a family.
11. Bake a dessert together.
12. Go caroling together.
13. Go to open space and play a sport together.
14. If you have a dog, take it for a long walk and take note of all the insects and plants you see.
15. Go on a short hike to a waterfall.

HYGGE HOBBIES

A hygge hobby is anything that offers you stress relief and comfort. You should engage in hobbies that bring you into the present, letting you forget your worries and stress. The more engaging and absorbing a hobby is, the more mindful it will make you. Try things like yoga, jogging, knitting, embroidering, painting, or hiking to achieve the rather Zen state of hygge. Anything you enjoy is good for you to incorporate into your life.

HYGGE AND TRAVEL

The Danish love to travel. This is for a good reason. Taking in the world around you and appreciating the experiences travel brings you is essential to being happy. If your budget allows you to, try to travel as much as you can.

Many Americans associate travel with stress. To be truly hygge about travel, you want to take it slow and enjoy your time abroad. Don't plan every moment, but instead let experiences happen as they will. Not everything needs to be perfect, and often plans fall apart so don't expect to strictly follow them. Instead, wake up each morning, decide what you want to do, and do it. Tailor experiences to your preferences.

You should also maximize your comfort. Bring a neck pillow on planes or long car rides, as well as a soft, plush blanket.

Many people fail to plan for a cold draft on planes or buses, so be sure to bring warm socks and a comfortable sweatshirt. Sleep when you can. You may consider bringing your own pillow and blanket to help you sleep in unfamiliar rooms. Bring the items you need to feel at home, such as hand sanitizer, a spray that smells like home, or headphones to listen to music that soothes you. While it is great to try new foods, you should also bring comfort foods that remind you of a home in case your stomach doesn't agree with the foreign foods.

Be sure to stay within budget. There is nothing quite like financial insecurity to ruin the pleasure of travel. It's acceptable to stay at a budget hostel or motel instead of breaking the bank for a five-star hotel when you'll be out and about for most of the day anyway. Taking the train or bus can be cheaper and less stressful than driving. There is no need to splurge on first class when the coach is perfectly functional. Find ways to save money and shop deals on sites like Travelzoo or Sherman's Travels.

Picking beautiful destinations is key. You want to enjoy traveling and enjoy the world around you. Experiencing new things and beautiful places will help you feel hygge immensely.

CHAPTER 11:

21 DAYS OF HYGGE CHALLENGE

Now that you have read up on everything you need to know about living the hygge way, we want to leave you with a challenge. This is a challenge to try 21 days of living this way. Think of it as slowly starting a diet, trying one new aspect of hygge each day. This way, you will not only ease into this new happy lifestyle and begin to see the changes it is making inside of you, but it will also show you which parts of hygge work best for you. You can then plan going forward.

So, it's time to go get a calendar and choose at least one thing each day to try. You could do this however you want— by increasing the number of things you do each day as the weeks go on, or just trying one brand new practice each of the 21 days. Get your family involved and have fun with it! You'll already be fulfilling the hygge principle of togetherness.

21 WAYS TO INCORPORATE HYGGE INTO YOUR DAILY LIFE

1. A night without screens and tech
2. Bake bread from scratch
3. Bring something from outdoors inside (rocks, flowers, nature décor)

4. Have a movie night with friends and family
5. Find a quiet, comfortable place and read a book
6. Have a relaxing stay-in-your-pajamas day
7. Have breakfast in bed
8. Take a stroll through a park or nature preserve
9. Start a gratitude journal
10. Use candlelight instead of electricity for a night
11. Watch the sun rise or set
12. Have a warm drink at a quiet café with an old friend
13. Have a hot chocolate night with the family
14. Give yourself an at-home spa day with natural scrubs and soaps
15. Try beginner yoga (you can use videos from the internet and not spend money on an actual class at a studio!)
16. Hug everyone you care about
17. Listen to calming music
18. Take a walk around the neighborhood in sweatpants and a comfortable shirt
19. Hold hands with your spouse or other loved one while watching a movie
20. Lay in bed and talk to someone
21. Color in an adult coloring book

CHAPTER 12:

BEYOND THE 21-DAY CHALLENGE

Hygge does not just stop after you check off the activities on the list above. Besides, once you practice the hygge lifestyle for three weeks, you won't want to return to your typical hectic and unhappy routine. You can take hygge beyond the 21 days challenge in the previous chapter and make it a permanent fixture of your life.

Remember that hygge is about living in the moment, so forcing hygge and worrying about how to achieve it is counterproductive. Instead, just make an effort to enjoy at least one moment of your day. Soon, this will become such an ingrained habit that you won't even have to think about it. You will want to do it naturally so it won't take any work on your part.

Make an effort to take care of yourself. Take a few minutes to relax at least once a day. You owe it to yourself to be more hygge in your attitude and your routine. Not every moment will be comfortable or enjoyable; you can't always forget about your worries and cares. But if you do it at least once a day, you will enjoy life so much more than you do now.

Be sure to make gratitude a daily habit. Keep a gratitude journal and tell your loved ones you appreciate them.

Also, make your home and workplace a hygge atmosphere. This will help you enjoy life more. When you change your décor and wardrobe to be more comfortable, you will have fewer distractions and discomforts plaguing your day and ruining your mood.

Try to set up a pleasant morning routine to set the mood for the day ahead. Don't watch upsetting news stories on TV or scroll through glamorous posts on social media that fill you with envy. Don't hit the ground running, already burning energy in a hectic dash to get out the door in time. Instead, enjoy yourself. Wake up early and do some yoga or sip some tea without a feeling of anxiety and panic. Enjoy a leisurely breakfast with your loved ones. Get ready and enjoy the physical sensations of showering, getting dressed, doing your hair, and applying makeup. Try to take in the sunrise and the birdsong of early morning.

Getting your friends and family on board can help you make your life more hygge as well. You can all enjoy the precious moments together while leaving out distractions like phones and TV.

CHAPTER 13:

FURTHERING YOUR HAPPINESS

As the title of the book suggests, all of these types and all of this information is aimed at helping you find happiness in the chaotic world we live in. Happiness is something many of us, even in privileged societies, find ourselves chasing. However, the chase may be exactly what is making us unhappy. With hygge, you can slow down and find happiness and peace in the simple pleasures, which is a feeling that cannot be bought. Living the Danish way can be a rewarding experience for the whole family. So, remember to be grateful and cozy and spend time together.

LIVING LAGOM:

A Swedish Guide to a Balanced Life

CHAPTER 1

WHAT IS LAGOM?

Lagom (pronounced [là:gɔm]) is a Swedish word used to describe the perfect state when something is neither too much, nor too little. It is just enough to make you satisfied. It can be used when talking about anything from the weather to how much milk you pour in your coffee. If the question starts with "How much?" the typical answer in Sweden is "lagom." There are a few words that can be used as synonyms for lagom; for example, enough, moderate, and balanced. Despite being perfectly good words they don't, however, correspond exactly to the true meaning of lagom as a way to express when something is just enough. Although, they might be used to create an understanding of the interpretations of lagom.

Etymologists say lagom is a composition of the two words "lag" and "om." Centuries ago, when there was a lack of food, there was only one plate containing food and had to be enough to go around the table. No one at the table could take much food. In Swedish "lag" means "team" or in this case "table" and "om" means "around." Lagom is, therefore, said to imply a meaning of *around the table.* This explanation makes sense, although, nowadays, historians and etymologists say this is a myth and perhaps have been constructed later on to explain why the Swedish used the word lagom to begin with.

Lagom is used to describe when we are satisfied, or when something is enough. We all have a different perception of when we are contempt and satisfied. The definition might be a bit difficult to define, but this is the essence of lagom. There is no general description of how much lagom is, which makes it quite a complicated word. There are as many definitions for lagom as there areSwedish. How much each one considers to be satisfying is, of course, a matter of taste, and it can be difficult even for the Swedish to understand what someone else considers to be lagom. Of course, it is a constant source of discussion amongst friends, families, and couples when one of them wants lagom and gets either too much or too little. This is due to the giver that has not bothered to ask how much the receiver consider to be lagom. It is easy to give someone else what we ourselves believe to be the right amount. Frequent misunderstandings are expected, especially in the beginning defining each other's definition and taste, according to lagom. However, the misunderstandings are neither serious nor the source of any huge conflict at all amongst the Swedish. These difficulties regarding definition are so common in Sweden that no one really thinks about it, it is a part of everyday life. And it seems that there is no real definition of the word and there lies a silent agreement the Swedish have agreed to disagree on the definition and accept that everyone thinks differently.

If there is no real definition of lagom, then why use it? Is it not confusing and weird? To non-Swedish, the definition is weird and complicated, and it can be debated whether anything is lagom. Everyone has their own definition, and it is a matter of the fact that Swedish people tend to complain more about some things, like temperature. With constant complaints about the weather being too hot or too cold, too windy or too still, too much snow or not snowy enough, it seems like there is no real use for the word lagom. At least not while talking about the Swedish topic of choice -weather.

Distinguishing lagom is like comparing food that is too hot or not hot enough; too sweet or not sweet enough; so on. Despite these constant complaints the Swedish harbor, they are quite a contempt with everything when asked seriously. Perhaps these minor complaints are a way for the Swedish people to connect to each other and start a conversation. They might be on to something. Accepting things is being lagom instead of perfect, a source of happiness some things never being quite lagom. From this aspect, it is not about a useless word, but a useful and satisfying one that makes the Swedish happy with the condition about things.

The question still remains: Why is lagom something to strive for if we are not able to agree on what lagom is?

It is complicated to see the reasons why when lagom cannot have a proper definition. But, there is one more aspect of what the point of lagom might be, we have not talked about yet. If we dropped the importance to define lagom, then the whole point is that there is *no* definition. Perhaps the whole point of lagom is to figure out what it is for you and live accordingly without being so concerned with what other people think about lagom. Let's explain this further. In Sweden, the general mentality is each to his own. In other words, don't interfere in other people's lives when they have not asked for it, like letting them express their opinions and live life on their terms. Lagom is something that needs to be figured out independently and then applied to life. There is no right or wrong definition of lagom; it is a grey middle that is defined independently and expressed differently to each person. The aspect of lagom and its definition is beautiful because it holds space for interpretation for each person.

Lagom cannot be defined as one single, universal statement,

but an independent one that each individual has to define on their own. Lagom is adaptable to life and each person and can make it entirely your own according to your beliefs without being concerned what anyone else will say. As your life and your perspective change, so can your definition of lagom. Lagom is always in tune with you.

CHAPTER 2

LAGOM IN SWEDEN AND AROUND THE WORLD

In this second chapter, how do the Swedish people view lagom as they sometimes have a different view than the rest of the world. Since there is a difference in how the Swedish and others view lagom, let's take a closer look at these differences and the fascination of this worldwide phenomenon.

The Swedish have a somewhat complicated relationship with the word lagom and all that it stands for. The lagom lifestyle is a way of thinking and acting is deeply internalized in the Swedish way of being, and they don't tend to think about it. It is a life that goes on and on in a nice little rut of decisions, and the fact that it does makes lagom go by unnoticed, perhaps even ignored. On the contrary, other Swedish are sick and tired being labeled as lagom. They feel stuck in a rut and tend to feel ashamed being considered moderate, never too much, too loud and so on, seizing every opportunity trying to break free. It is not easy to explain why some Swedish have this feeling. Perhaps they don't want to be labeled and want to break free from the term. Others just ignore or live with the label that has been imposed on them.

Despite the anti-lagom , Swedish people, in general, are more careful to keep their lives lagom-style than living too large or putting themselves in a situation where they are noticed. The Swedish can be regarded as contempt being labeled lagom as they live their lagom lives. Perhaps some of them have become more comfortable with being lagom now when the rest of the world is picking up this trend as well. Sometimes it is easier to see the greatness once more people notice it.

The struggles with the definition mentioned in the previous chapter, the Swedish complicated relationship with this word, is a fact that many countries are becoming more and more fascinated by this phenomenon. And, it is fascinating how a rather small country like Sweden influences others to live a different kind of life in order to maintain balance. Some Swedish state that they maintain the lagom lifestyle because they find it is the easiest way to live a sustainable, healthy, happy and balanced life. Some of them consider lagom to be the perfect interstitial path in a divided world full of contradictions and non-consequent advice. Lagom allows you to enjoy all the little pleasures in life and still be healthy and satisfied.

To the rest of the world, lagom seems to be a clever way to make a difference in the world and turn certain events around in order to make things better. In a world where we face huge environmental issues and are in a constant search of ways to save the planet, lagom might, in fact, impose a more sustainable lifestyle. For example, instead of buying food that goes uneaten, buy enough to last a certain time before going grocery shopping again. This goes for clothes and everything else as well, buy what you need and what you use and leave the rest. To the rest of the world, lagom might be a way to describe that we don't want to buy more than we use and when we do buy something consider the quality over quantity aspect. This can save you time and money in the long run. This is also applicable to the work and home balance many of us struggle with. Instead of working too much and spending little time with our children, strive to do everything lagom-style to make time for both the business and pleasures in life without facing a burnout. These are some of the reasons why the world is fascinated and inspired by Sweden and lagom.

While some of the Swedish people are sick and tired of being caught in this grey scale of life where everything is lagom, in moderation and just enough to satisfy them and longing for some glamour and flair, the rest of the world are turning their eyes to Sweden as a leading example of a sustainable, healthy and happy lifestyle. So maybe the Swedish are just too self-critical and bored by the rut they are stuck in to see their own greatness and the inspiration they bring to the table and how they can actually take the lead in making things better for this planet.

CHAPTER 3

LAGOM, HAPPINESS, AND HYGGE

We have already touched how lagom can be connected to happiness and how it can lead to a more harmonious life. In this chapter, we dig deeper in the hope of discovering more about this. In this book, when we raise the subject of lagom and its connection to happiness, keep in mind that we don't talk about happiness as this feeling in your stomach before waking up on Christmas day or hearing the footsteps outside of your door in the morning of your birthday as a child or the happiness of receiving something you have long longed for. Instead, it is a subtle and calm feeling of happiness. A happiness that does not yell at you or is overwhelming but happiness that is rising from a place of satisfaction.

Although some groups of the Swedish population are trying to break free from being labeled as lagom, Sweden has paved the way for a new way of achieving balance and also more happiness. Settling for lagom when you could be striving for more is not a bad idea. In fact, the Swedish are definitely on to something. By settling for lagom they don't take on more responsibilities than they are able to and doing so, they apply some sort of self-preservation and self-care. When settling occurs in your job and your life, there is no urgency to strive for more for yourself or for your family. Use the time to do things you enjoy that creates happiness. Working constantly is not healthy for you, your mind or your family as your energy from work has been depleted. Applying moderation in your life will create happiness and can increase the amount of happiness already present in your life.

To accomplish lagom, consider to take a look at your life and analyze what is important to you. Take a look at your habits and see how they can improve. And what better way to use some extra time than to create things that make you happy? What makes us happy is individual, but whatever you like to do, using lagom in your life will make some time for your favorite things. It is important to remember that time is not the only connection between lagom and happiness -- it is contempt. Considering things to be "just good enough" rather than striving for perfection can save plenty of irritations and help you to a stress-free life. Maybe not at first. During the first efforts of changing your way of thinking into lagom can be frustrating as things can begin to pile up and not be completed. It is like quitting smoking or caffeine. It is frustrating, and you might have abstinence from things, but after a while, happiness will come easier to you than before.

Talking about lagom and about happiness there is another phenomenon worth mentioning. In Denmark, they have a thing called hygge [pronounced hoo-ga]. Hygge can be described as a warm, cozy and comfortable atmosphere where you take your time to enjoy the good things in life with the people you love. Hygge is an activity, or a state of being, as lagom is a view on life and a way of living. However different, there is a connection to be found between hygge and lagom. They are both derived from a longing of slowing down and keeping things simple. Lagom is all about balance and moderation, and when having hygge, you are spending your time in a moderate way. It is an easy-going atmosphere where nothing is too much or too little, but just lagom. Therefore, hygge is a lagom state of being, despite the lack of connection overall. While lagom and hygge are different connections to living and feeling, they lie in cause and consequence. Applying lagom to your life to achieve balance, to find more time for the things you love to do. This extra time saved can be spent with family, friends and other loved ones, and hobbies in a cozy atmosphere called hygge. It all works out as a circle of being cozy and happy in your home as energy and money should not be wasted to enjoy the time. In other words, hygge is lagom completely.

What hygge consists of is a matter of taste. To some people it might be meeting some friends over dinner, catching up after work in a nice coffee shop or a movie night with your family. The point of hygge is to be calm and cozy, to pass the time with where you will be energized instead of burning energy constantly. Filling up your energy like this will result in a balanced, happy and content life. Furthermore, enjoying the little things in life can improve your ability to handle a mediocre job, a mean colleague at work or any other small, annoying things that occur in your everyday life.

CHAPTER 4

LAGOM IN PERSONAL LIFE, FAMILY, AND RELATIONSHIPS

In the first three chapters, there are many definitions of how lagom is connected to an increase in time, money and happiness in life. Discover how you can achieve these things in your life. We are going to cover the subject on how to apply lagom to your personal life, spending time with family, friends, and others, and how these actions could lead to better relationships with yourself and those around you. Plus, learn to set aside time and energy to enjoy special interests and hobbies.

Today, we are encouraged from a young age to be social; spend time with others and working well in a group is a characteristic that is encouraged and rewarded in today's society. Why this has become increasingly important is hard to find, but social skills are just as important as any other competence when looking for a job. Although, social skills and the importance of communicating well is not a new trend in itself. Guidelines for good people skills can be found in the New Testament. In Peter 4:8-9, we can find the following: "Above all, maintain constant love for one another, for love covers a multitude of sins. Be hospitable to one another without complaining". Social skills have been important for ages, but it is more important today as many people are competing for the same jobs with the same competence. With the influence of technology, online marketing and social networks online, it is even more important to stay social in order to be noticed and successful. Even during spare time, staying connected to social media isn't ideal for resting as it keeps the stress and mind alert. For some reason, being introverted and enjoying time alone and offline is almost considered a handicap, and there are even therapy and courses to teach us how to overcome this behavior and become more social. It is a challenge to stay balanced and disconnect once in a while when the world around is encouraging us to be online and connected constantly.

The Swedish, however, have a reputation of being somewhat cold and distant to strangers and to each other despite the want and need for social skills in their society. But, the Swedish are not really anti-social. Most of them are just as social as everyone else, but they inherited the mindset of leaving each to his own, combined with their lagom lifestyle, gives them an air of solitude-seeking and loneliness in their life. The Swedish behavior is actually quite healthy and something for the rest of us to adopt. In western society, we are forced to be social at work, in school and wherever we spend our time during the day. Sometimes the expectations are on high-demand for us to deliver when it comes to being social throughout the day. Spending time with family, work or study with classmates and teachers, and still expected to be cordial with our colleagues can be stressful and exhaust our energy levels. In the evening it is still expected from others and society to be social on days off when all our bodies need is sleep and rest. Filling up days things to do within the week leads to exhaustion and lost interests and passions in life. When transitioning to the lagom lifestyle, you might get frustrated and even hate doing things you usually enjoy with others just because you have been forced into everything and forced away from yourself.

Therefore, it is important to keep in touch with yourself and your own interests in order to enjoy all of these social events that are quite nice when you find the balance.

In Sweden, when people sit alone on the bus or avoid talking to each other while waiting in line at the supermarket, they are creating a balance between social commitments recovery time. It is true that the Swedish are keener on minding their own business than many others and contributes to their lagom lifestyle. They can chat with the person next to them, but they don't because of value space and privacy. In these situations, lagom does not mean staying at the house, locking yourself inside and have scheduled time alone because that does not work. Instead, lagom is about being quiet while riding the bus or standing in line. It is not the perfect scheduled downtime alone but rather a good compromise to recharge and have more energy once you get home to your family. By applying lagom this way, the Swedish have cracked the code of balance between being social and being alone. Instead of bending over backward trying to keep up with all the social events and commitments, the Swedish people take care of their alone time. They spend time alone by themselves or with their family allowing the time to recover and recharge. Because being social can lead to frustration and exhaustion.

Once you take the time to rearrange your busy schedule and recharge properly, it is possible that you will want to take up a hobby. Hobbies are often the first to get crossed of the lists as we become busy with work and family. Although, hobbies are good for the well-being and having a thing you love is relaxing and recharging in itself. As discussed earlier, applying lagom leads to an increased amount of free time that you can use to recharge. Recharging energy levels can bring love and joy to the hobbies once loved. The love and joy you find in a hobby also generate new energy that you need for work and family. Of course, a hobby can be social, but by being alone, you can do only what you feel like. Your mind can rest for a moment, and you can go deep within and follow your voice. Lagom is about balance, and if you are usually very social, this is a way to find balance.

On the other hand, if you are anti-social and prefer spending time alone, lagom might mean that you should put yourself out there more. Maybe create time to spend with friends, family, and others. If you are generally anti-social at work, try talking to your colleagues and ask them questions to spark conversation. Meeting new people outside of work like joining a group or join an association to share like-minded interests. Meeting new people can bring fulfillment in life and enjoy life experiences.

Finding a balance between work and home life can be hard to accomplish but is completely possible. If you find yourself working yourself hard with no time left for pleasure or find yourself complaining about the workload, then you might want to take a look at the solution you are able to control. The solution may not always be there, but by thinking about your options and asking friends, family or co-workers for help, a solution will arise. If you can, maybe talk to your boss about having too much on your hands, say no to colleagues who want help when you are too busy for your own work. Or, help each other out to succeed at the same goal. If you find that you are working at a dead-end, try to find a new job or a new career. Everything is possible to achieve balance in your life.

Sorting out your priorities can be hard. To find the lagom balance, write a list of things you feel like you have to do and write a list of things you want to enjoy doing. Then, prioritize the list of things you have to do and would like to do, putting them in order starting with the most important. Throughout the day, cross them off as you go. The key here is doing a little of what has to be done and would like to enjoy doing. At the end of the day, both lists will have things crossed off to see what was accomplished. This will leave you feeling satisfied and contempt how the day was spent. In other words, doing more with the time you have to enjoy a moment of hygge with family and friends.

The Swedish are not better than anyone else at saying no, prioritizing and enjoying relationships and hobbies. Although they do have the concept of lagom, they don't think about what they can do on their days off to spend time with their families and friends. Perhaps the Swedish have a more natural longing for solitude than others, helping them to stay balanced in their social engagements.

Lagom is a lifestyle to achieve balance within yourself and in your life. Spending time with family and friends and enjoying hobbies and interests alone is important to your health and mind. Do everything well enough instead of striving for perfection; no one will thank you for working yourself hard than settling for a little less. Do not feel guilty for not giving your all and most important think of lagom in the sense of doing everything in moderation and for balance. If you have worked too much, then make sure to spend some time at home, if you have been social a lot then try to have some alone time. And so on.

How much should you have of everything in order to have balance? Depends how much you should work, be alone, socialize, etc. is up to you to decide. If you love your job and don't have anyone waiting at home, then spend more time at work. If you recharge by being surrounded by people, then spend more time with others while an introvert may need more time alone to feel balanced. Think about your wants, needs and what you have to do and see what can be rearranged to achieve that balance in life the lagom way. Everything in moderation and remember that a little of everything is better than nothing of some and too much of others.

CHAPTER 5

LAGOM AT HOME

Lagom is not only useful for creating harmony and balance between work and life or between socializing and time alone; it is a useful tool to make your home a peaceful, relaxing and comfortable space to dwell in. In this chapter, focus on creating the most peaceful home you have ever had the lagom way.

Starting with the home itself and its decorations, there are a plethora of things to make it a cozy and comfortable place to be. Do you have any furniture not being used by you, your family, or guests? Start with that. Filter out the furniture that is never used to eliminate the clutter and fill your home with decorations you love, and that brings you joy and happiness. Then continue on, eliminating decorations, cushions, and curtains you don't like, use or fit in your home.

Home is a place to relax, spend time with your family and escape from all your social engagements, work, and demands from people outside. Having a home that has things you love it can bring joy, confidence, and happiness to you and others around you. Having a cluttered home can be overwhelming, which can bring stress to your life instead of relaxation. Remember that you owe your things, not the other way around.

The moment your things become cluttered, and they serve no

use to you or the house's function, it is time to start decluttering and achieve Zen. Zen is an eastern philosophy that originated in Buddhism. In our western culture, it has come to reflect a calm and meditative state of being. There is no obvious connection between lagom and Zen, but when applying lagom and decluttering your home, you can reach a calm and satisfying state where you owe your things without being overwhelmed. When reaching Zen by living lagom, you will also feel more energized and less stressed. Despite the lack of connection between this two phenomenon and philosophies, lagom is a useful technique if you want to achieve zen. In search of a peaceful, happy and rich life, lagom, as well as zen, are powerful tools to use. Furthermore, Zen is a well-known and popular philosophy, and by connecting lagom to Zen and letting them work together, may give a wider perspective in the world.

When it comes to things, it is not better to have more. In fact, many things only give you more to clean, more to replace when broken or worn out and you will probably spend more time searching for things you have replaced and cannot find anymore. You should absolutely have what you need, but don't fill your home with nice things only to have them full or to show off to occasional visitors. Instead, try to adopt a less is more approach to your home. How much things your home should contain is up to you as it is a matter of need and taste. Feel free to have curtains, cushions, a wine glass collection and those nice and expensive dinner plates you only use for Christmas, but take a look at your life and what you really need, what you think you need, and how much of everything you need. Don't forget to only keep and buy things you truly love and care for. Even if you need an item, don't keep it if it does not make you smile. Sell the old one, or give it away and invest in a piece that makes you smile instead. Remember, the definition of lagom is up to you and differ from person to person.

Many people say they need more storage space or smart solutions to store things in the already existing storage areas of their homes, but what most people actually need is to clean out their spaces and sort out what to keep and what to get rid of. A home that is cluttered-free is more harmonious, and you can come home from work feeling relaxed and comfortable instead of your home flooded with things you need to organize and clean. Of course, decluttering your home takes work, and it can take a long time before you are completely done, but once your home is properly organized and neat, you will find yourself at peace. There is always something to declutter like that junk draw in the kitchen or bedroom, or underneath the sinks are perfect places to clean out and organize. Who knows, the process could become a hobby you enjoy to do.

Another cluttered mess that can impact the home environment and your life is your wardrobe. Getting dressed in the morning can be both pleasure and torture. Many of us are sick and tired of looking at our clothes and thinking that we have nothing to wear. Decluttering your wardrobe the lagom way can get rid of this anxiety-driven nightmare.

Begin by emptying your closet. This is not something you have to do; it is recommended to see the clothes you have and get a good picture of the state your current wardrobe is in. Then, pick up one item at the time and consider how much you like this item, how much you can identify with it and how useful it is in your everyday life. Only keep the things you use, love and feel are right for you. It is not necessary to make it into a complete capsule wardrobe with a limited amount of pieces. The point is to keep it organized and simple so that you have a wardrobe that expresses your personality and where you can easily find the perfect combination for each occasion, where the clothes fit together nicely and are made in materials of good quality.

After you have organized your current wardrobe and gotten rid of things you don't want, write a list of things you need to complement the rest of your wardrobe. Another great tip regarding clothes and is easy, plan out your outfits for the week ahead saving you time and agony in the morning. The Swedish uses lagom to simplify their wardrobe and their lives as they have more time making and eating a nice breakfast instead.

We have talked about our homes and wardrobes, but how can you shop the lagom way? The Swedish love to shop, but they are conscious buyers. Being a conscious buyer is to buy only what you need, considering quality over quantity and always follow your taste. The perfect way to buy what you only need is making a list. It does not matter if you are buying decorations for your home, clothes or food --think about what you need and write a list (the Swedish love lists). Also, avoid impulse buying. If faced with a situation where you are standing in a store wanting to buy something, consider its use in your life. If you cannot come up with one, walk away. Also, think about quality over quantity so items can last longer when it comes to clothes, furniture, and decorations. This way you buy fewer things you will enjoy for a longer time.

When shopping with moderation, think twice before buying anything. It may seem dull to shop the lagom way, but it can be delightful spending time looking for one perfect, thoughtful item then multiple not-so-good items. This will save you time and money, and become happier with each buy than before. Before shopping, consider the following questions:

- Do I need this item?
- When will I use it? Think of at least one specific moment in the near-future when you will wear or use this item.

- Can I afford this? Don't consider the price tag; consider how many times you can wear or use this piece. An expensive thing can cost less than a budget alternative if used more frequently than the cheaper option.
- Do I want this for myself or is it something I want because everyone else has it? Only buy things you want; don't buy anything because someone else says so.
- Do I already have this or something similar at home to use instead?
- Will I be able to sell this when I no longer find it useful? Even if you are uncertain about a buy, determine if it can be resold later on. By selling things for someone else to use saves money and incorporates sustainable living habits.

Sometimes an impulse can meet the criteria's of a good bargain. If faced with an impulse buy, after using the questions above, use this trick: Take a picture of it. Go home and sleep on it. If you are still thinking about the item can envision its functionality in your home or life, then can buy it. Most of the time we don't crave these impulses the next day, but if we do, it may be a good item to buy.

Buying the lagom way can bring happiness, joy, and comfort to you and others around you. Less things mean more space and time. More space means that your home will be easier to clean and to keep things tidy on a daily basis. Now, you will have more time for other hobbies or interests because you're not spending time cleaning. A wardrobe that is simple and easier to choose from will leave more time and energy for the day. Less things mean more money. Selling the things you don't want to keep and earn extra money is sustainable. Decluttering your home will make it appear open, neat, and clean for guests and yourself.

All of these things save you energy and time doing things you love with the people you love. Declutter, stay organized and find suitable solutions to keep your habitat tidy to turn your home into a relaxing and calm place where you find peace and recharge.

CHAPTER 6

LAGOM HEALTH
AND WELL BEING

Discussing the impact of lagom when applying it to relationships, life, and home can help decrease stress and increase time, money and energy for things you want to enjoy. Lagom is not always about the materialistic relics in your home or how you feel in social outings; it can affect how you feel within yourself: your well-being.

In Sweden, people like to move their bodies not because they need to achieve anything but because of how it makes them feel both in their mind and in their bodies. They love the feeling of movement in their bodies, which is one more reason for them to exercise. Swedish people might not be known for being the most competitive people when it comes to sports, but they do move frequently. They exercise everyday like taking walks and riding bikes instead of driving. They take the stairs instead of the elevator, and so on. The Swedish like to keep their bodies healthy. Marathon training, Viking races, and iron man races have become a trend lately for even the average Swede. Although these races are rather extreme, they have become increasingly popular, and it is a sign of the current trends. Despite the Swedish fascination for exercise and the impact it has on the body and mind, they are cautious not to overdo anything. Instead of exercising way too much for the perfect body, they work out in order to achieve the accomplishment itself and for the feel of it.

But not all Swedish are interested in these extreme workouts, and even those who are dedicated to them are careful not to stretch their bodies too much. They are careful to have lagom and balance between working out their bodies, their minds and relaxing all together. Exercising is something that needs fit into the work and life balance, and this can be challenging. To maintain a balance between activity and rest as well as between work and life and instead of having only the toughest workouts, they go for a hike in the forest for a day or do something else that balances exercise with family life while still bringing tranquility. You can definitely have a balance and still keep up with an exercise routine.

Hiking and doing things with your family can be considered relaxing while still being physical activity. It is relaxing because you don't just work your body, your brain gets a mental rest while enjoying a hygge moment with family in the forest or by the sea. This can also aid in recovery and boost energy levels.

In general, the Swedish love spending time in nature. It does not matter if they are going for a run, spending the day with their kids in the park or spending sunny summer days by the sea swimming and tanning. Spending time outside can boost your body in more than one way with staying active and delivering much-needed vitamins to the skin. Most of the time we are indoors working, studying, or spending time alone or with others, we forget how much our bodies need to stay active.

Health and well-being are not all about physical exercise. It is relaxing and exercises the mind. We spend our days with a lot of impressions, and it is hard sometimes to tune out and let the mind rest for a moment. In Sweden, meditation, mindfulness, and yoga have become increasingly popular in order to balance the hectic life. Not everyone loves meditation, and all people certainly don't love yoga, but the fine thing is that doing what the Swedish do when being in nature, saying no to certain events to be with family and recover is to be considered mindfulness and gives life a nice touch of lagom.

Another movement in Sweden where more and more people are moving to the countryside, buying a cabin outside of town and gardening has kicked up popularity and can be relaxing and satisfying for the mind. This can be considered a reaction to make the hectic life more lagom. There are several ways to create balance and find some peace of mind in our daily lives. Remember, lagom everything.

Closely related to the subject of health and exercise is what you eat. As far as food is considered, the Swedish try to prioritize eating solid home-cooked meals made with clean and healthy ingredients as possible. They prefer to eat with their families, and to most people in Sweden, good food is important to the overall well-being. They do eat junk food moderately but shy away from microwaveable dinners or anything containing chemicals. They use real butter despite the calories than eating light products that contain additives that are generally not good for your health. It is easy to find and buy organic food, and they are dedicated to buying locally produced food to support small businesses and avoid the long transportations of food. Food transportations take time so that the food is not fresh once it reaches the store. The transportations contribute to pollution, and the Swedish prefer to buy local. Locally produced food is like a quality stamp that guarantees the food is of good quality, costing more than average, the Swedish like to support their local farmers. They love to eat good food, but in the true sense of lagom they do not only want it to taste good, but they also want it to be healthy.

In Sweden, the National Food Agency (NFA), provides guidelines on how to eat to get all of the important nutrients the body needs. It is a discussion amongst the Swedish if they should be trusted or not since some of their advice is contradictory to certain peoples believes regarding what is to be considered healthy food. This is not a proven fact, but in Sweden, people following specific diets, for example, Paleo and LCHF dislike that the NFA recommends the Swedish to eat plenty of pasta, bread, and other carbs. Some trust them, and some don't, but whether you trust these guidelines or not, they are created to help people live healthy lives, by recommending a diet containing both vegetables, fruits, carbs, fats, and proteins. The NFA guidelines state to fill at least a third of your plate (preferably half of it) with vegetables and/or fruits. But, the Swedish love their traditional dishes. They are also curious about trying new things and are not afraid to mix things up with influences from different corners of the world.

Finding healthy food that is not chemically treated, organic and locally produced is easy in Sweden. You can find these foods both in the local supermarkets and in local farmers markets. If you are insecure or don't have time to grocery shop, they have different websites like Blue Apron and Hello Fresh, where you can order your groceries online to be delivered straight home along with healthy recipes. There is something to fit every food choices in your life: vegan food, vegetarian, easy to cook food, and grocery bags with organic food if you would prefer that. The Swedish people strive to live the lagom way regarding their health. And if you might find these concepts new and time-consuming, the Swedish people do it quite effortlessly since they incorporate several of these things together. For example, they relax from work by spending time outside with their families, and while doing this, they get exercise, relaxation and family time all wrapped up in one. They cook a delicious and healthy meal and eat with their family. As a bonus, to make it easier for you to start living the lagom way, there recipes in the next chapter.

CHAPTER 7

LAGOM IN THE KITCHEN

To continue the health and lifestyle the lagom way, here are some classical Swedish recipes to try at home. As an added bonus, we included some non-Swedish recipes that they love and fit their lagom lifestyle. There will be tips on how to make your own junk food, since making things yourselves will make it healthier, and you can add healthy choices to otherwise unhealthy meals. This way you will get a nice overall view of how lagom can be applied practically to all aspects of life.

Before we get started, it is necessary to point out these recipes have been slightly altered. We had added some veggies to classical recipes because when these dishes became popular, the Swedish did not have access to many vegetables due to the cold and difficult climate. Today, fruits and vegetables are imported, and the use of greenhouses have become popular that access to these ingredients is easier to obtain than ever before. The Swedish now eat more veggies, salads, and fruits along with their meats and starches. With that said, the traditional recipes are not really healthy and have been adapted as access to vegetables and other ingredients have become easier to obtain.

There are a few recipes for breakfast, lunch, and dinner that the Swedish love to eat. As a bonus, we will share tips for healthier desserts and snacks the Swedish people love.

BREAKFAST

Breakfast is considered the most important meal, especially in Sweden. It is common to eat cereals or granola with milk or yogurt, sandwiches, and porridge. Although there has been an increasing trend in eating overnight oats or drinking a smoothie, the traditional breakfast dishes are still the most popular ones. Here we share a recipe for simple granola that you can add your favorite flavors too and modify to your taste. You also get easy to make oatmeal porridge that will give you enough energy to last all the way to lunch without having your blood sugar levels sinking too low.

Homemade granola with yogurt

Ingredients

Mixed nuts (neutral, not roasted or salted)	Sunflower seed
	Honey or maple syrup
Oatmeal	Olive oil
Coconut flakes	Cinnamon
Flaxseed	Cardamom

Directions

1. Mix all the dry ingredients together on an ovenproof dish.
2. Mix in some olive oil and honey or maple syrup.
3. Season it and let it dry in the oven at a low temperature during 30-45 minutes, don't forget to open the oven and mix the granola a couple of times while it is drying. Otherwise, it might burn on top and still be moist in the bottom.

If you are allergic to nuts, you can add some other grains and seeds. If you don't like cinnamon or cardamom, you can use other spices of your choice. Leave to cool down before putting it in a jar. Add dried fruits such as raisins, apricots or cranberries once the granola is dried and cold for a fruity flavor and added benefits.

Oatmeal porridge

Ingredients

1 part oatmeal
2 parts water
A pinch of salt

Directions

This one is so easy it is fail-proof, and anyone can do it.

1. Take one part oatmeal and two parts water, add a pinch of salt and cook until the porridge is firm but not glue-like. If it is too lose then cook it some more; if it is too hard or has the same texture as glue, add more water and stir.
2. Serve the porridge with fresh fruits and berries and milk, if you like. Use almond milk, coconut milk, or lactose-free milk for a dairy-free alternative.

SANDWICHES

If you-you'd a sandwich eater for breakfast, here are some healthier lagom alternatives. In fact, the sandwich is not a bad option since it is versatile and you can make anything with a sandwich. Use sourdough bread and fill it with a wide range of healthier options like hummus or cream cheese instead of butter topped with your favorite vegetables. Or, use a cream cheese spread and add cold chicken, some green leafs such as spinach leaves or arugula leaves, tomato with a yogurt dressing to make it moist. The options are endless.

If you prefer having eggs in the morning eat up. Eggs are an excellent source of protein and good fats. Plus, the Swedish eat a ton of eggs, boiled or fried, or poached to put on a sandwich. They also eat scrambled eggs and bacon for breakfast at times. Keep lagom in mind and eat everything in moderations; there really are no other rules here.

LUNCH AND DINNER

For lunch, the Swedish usually have leftovers from dinner the night before as they cook huge meals during the weekends and store the leftovers in the freezer or fridge to eliminate cooking lunch during the weekdays. Of course, some eat lunch out, but the average Swedish person brings leftovers to work. The Swedish children are served lunch in school, so they don't have to bring their own, but during weekends and holidays, the families usually eat a cooked meal at home. The lunch and dinner dishes are similar to all of these recipes can be served as either lunch or dinner. Of course, the Swedish do eat out, but not on a regular basis. In Sweden, eating out is to celebrate and indulge themselves than that is part of everyday life.

Classic Swedish Meatballs

This has to be the most famous and popular dish amongst Swedish recipes, and we could not leave this one out. It is a classic favorite dish in Sweden for a reason. Try it, and you will understand why. It is easy to make, tasty, and kids will love. Add vegetables for added health benefits.

Ingredients

The minced meat of your choice (beef, pork, or lamb)	Breadcrumbs
	Milk
	Butter or olive oil
Onion	Salt
Egg	Pepper

87

Directions

1. Mix the breadcrumbs with the milk and leave it to settle.
2. Chop or grate the onion into fine pieces.
3. Mix minced meat with the onion, egg, salt, and pepper. Mix it all together with a spoon or your hands.
4. Pour in some of the milk and breadcrumbs mixes and mix it in the meat. Keep adding milk and breadcrumbs until the blend has a nice texture. It should be soft to roll and the meatballs firm. Try to frying a meatball to see how it cooks. If it is too dry, it will crumble. Add more milk and breadcrumbs to the mixture.
5. Fry the meatballs in butter.

Serve the meatballs with boiled or mashed potatoes and brown sauce. Traditional meatballs are served with pickled cucumbers and lingonberry jam with grilled tomato, a mixed salad on the side, green beans, peas or broccoli.

Steak with oven roasted potatoes and béarnaise sauce

Another classic dish in Sweden that is popular in the summertime when you can have a barbecue, but it is also possible to make it inside the stow. This one is also easy to make.

Ingredients

A steak of your choice	Potatoes
Béarnaise (Homemade is	Olive oil
preferred but bought one	Salt
is nice also)	Pepper

Directions

1. Cut the potatoes in two or four, and season with olive oil, salt, pepper, and French herbs. Roast in the oven, 225 °C for about 30 minutes.

2. Season the steak with salt and pepper. Grill or fry steak.

Serve the steak with the béarnaise sauce and roasted potatoes. Serve with in-season vegetables along with grilled (or fried) tomatoes, asparagus or green beans. Add a mixed salad on the side, grilled (or fried) corn-cob or anything else you and your family like.

Homemade Béarnaise Sauce

Ingredients

2 Egg yolks	Pepper
Red wine vinegar	Estragon
100-gram butter	Parsley
Salt	

Directions

1. Mix egg yolks with some red wine vinegar.
2. Melt the butter and leave to rest.
3. Heat the eggs in a bowl above boiling water. Whisk it constantly.

When the eggs start to thicken, remove it from the heat and start adding the butter a little at the time while whisking constantly. When the sauce is nice and thick (you might not need all the butter) you add salt, pepper, and the herbs according to your taste.

Pasta carbonara

While pasta dishes are primarily Italian, but Swedish recipes have adopted them into their meals. A dish is pasta carbonara. This is not the actual original Italian recipe but is used in Sweden and can be altered to your tastes. Feel free to add more garlic, remove the parsley, use the entire egg instead of just the yolk and so on. Nothing can wrong in this recipe.

Ingredients

Spaghetti noodles	Garlic
Bacon	Salt
Cream (start with 1	Pepper
deciliter and add more if	Parsley
you want more sauce)	Egg yolk
Onion	

Directions

1. Boil the spaghetti.
2. Chop the onion, garlic, and bacon and fry together.
3. Add cream and seasonings.
4. Mix the spaghetti and egg yolk together with the bacon and cream mixture. Let it simmer. If you want more sauce, just add more cream.

Serve pasta on top of spinach leaves and add a side dish of chopped tomatoes with olive oil and salt.

Paned plaice file with mashed potatoes

Of course, we cannot exclude fish from the menu since Swedish people eat plenty of seafood. The key to all fish is to keep it simple. Like this plaice file. It is easy and tasty and most certainly a fail-proof dish to serve. If you can, try to get some fresh fish instead of frozen as it changes the taste entirely.

Ingredients

Plaice file (fresh or	Potatoes
frozen)	Milk
Breadcrumbs	Butter
Egg	

Directions

1. Beat the eggs in a bowl until blended together. Set aside.
2. Coat the plaice files in the egg mixture and bread it in the breadcrumbs; cover completely.
3. Fry the files in butter , about 3-5 minutes on each side.
4. Boil the potatoes and mash them with milk and butter to taste.

Serve the fish and mash potatoes with a slice of lemon and a mixed salad of your choice. We recommend green peas, Brussels sprouts, broccoli or if you have it at home you can serve it with ratatouille.

Toast Skagen

This toast is more of an entree dish, and it is so delicious we could not possibly leave it out. Skagen is a place located on the Swedish west coast, but it is unclear why this particular dish was named after it, perhaps it has something to do with the west coast in Sweden is most famous for its seafood. However, this toast is a delicacy served not only in the west coast but in restaurants all over Sweden.

Ingredients

Fresh shrimps, peeled	Crème Fraîche
Dill	Bread (preferably
Lemon	sourdough, but any kind
Horseradish	that you can fry will do)
Mayonnaise	A slice of butter

Directions

1. Mix the shrimps with dill, grated horseradish, mayonnaise and crème fraîche, all according to your liking.
2. Season with salt, pepper, and lemon to taste. Add more

seasoning if needed.

3. Fry the bread in the butter until it is golden brown. If the bread is soaking up the butter, add more. The pan is not supposed to run dry; this will burn the bread instead.

4. Put the mixture shrimps on the bread. Decorate the toast with a dill twig and a slice of lemon.

A few classical Swedish dishes that will make you satisfied without being too much. They are delicious and easy to make with the capability to add more vegetables for added health benefits. By trying out these recipes, it is easy to understand why the Swedish have extra time to do all the things they want and need to do to achieve lagom in their lives. These recipes are simple to prepare and cook, leaving more time for family than in the kitchen.

JUNK FOOD

The fact is that junk food cannot be completely erased out of our diets, even the Swedish. And we cannot write about lagom and food without mentioning junk food. How can enjoy junk food in a lagom way while still maintaining a healthy diet and lifestyle. Here are some tips that the Swedish use.

First and foremost try to keep the balance. If you eat healthy and well balanced most of the time, there is no reason why you should not enjoy junk food every once in a while. By all means, indulge yourself in a burger, fries and a milkshake moderately. Use the Swedish model of dining out and do it to spoil yourself instead of using fast food as a go to, everyday solution than cooking at home. We know that many junk food restaurants have begun serving healthier options, like carrot sticks instead of fries. But even in Sweden, the fries with the burger is a love relationship that can't be separated. The healthy and conscious

Swedish have figured out that if they eat healthy all the other days, they can enjoy junk food. Just don't let it happen on a daily basis.

Furthermore, burgers and pizza can be made at home and are easy to prepare. Even French fries can be healthy if made at home as the salt is controlled than at a fast-food place. Make sure to use clean ingredients without bad supplements or chemicals, and try to make the majority of the sauces and dough (for pizza) yourself. A homemade burger with pineapple, pickled onions, salad, and tomato, is not so bad. Besides, making them yourself will make you feel fuller faster and control how much you intake. Making your own fries by cutting potatoes and baking them with olive oil and salt in the oven instead of buying fries is a better and healthier alternative.

Making your own pizza is a healthier option, choosing fresh ingredients and control what goes in and on your pizza. Plus, it is a fun activity for the whole family to enjoy together.

It can be overwhelming cooking at home on most nights, but it is well worth the effort. In Sweden, gathering a few friends or family and cooking together is a great way to socialize.

SNACKS

In Sweden, it is recommended to eat three larger meals and two snacks each day. Eating breakfast, lunch, and dinner, plus two snacks between lunch and dinner. This helps regulate blood sugar levels to help maintain energy all day, eliminating the two o'clock crash and cravings. So, what is the Swedish snack of choice? It depends who you are asking and how old they are.

The younger children have something called a "fruit break" at school in the morning. Each child will have brought the fruit of choice in their school bag and eat their fruit as a class. Even at home, most children are served a fruit when they crave a little something between meals. Sometimes the children are served plain yogurt along with the fruit to keep the hunger at bay a while longer if needed.

For adults, two snacks are not necessary, and most will not eat that much. The adults who do eat two snacks in-between meals will eat a fruit or plain yogurt with fruit like the children. Other common snacks are a boiled egg, served with ham or another source of protein and/or a healthy sandwich. A smaller portion of the breakfast eaten as a snack or maybe a smoothie instead are popular options for a snack. The best of all is that these are all healthy and good options instead of consuming chocolate, a cookie or other sugary options. Of course, if you really crave a piece of chocolate, you can totally have a bite of that too. Just do it like the Swedish and choose at least 70% dark chocolate every so often; not every day.

It is about the balance when eating or adopting a lagom lifestyle. These changes will help you make better choices in more than one way. Snacking should be easy and easy to carry around with you, access it, and eat wherever.

The Swedish also enjoy coffee, in a lagom way. Drinking too much coffee is not good, but in Sweden, it is the obvious drink of choice even during snack time. So if you want to try snacking the Swedish style, combine healthy options with coffee, and you are on your way to eating the lagom way.

CHAPTER 8

LAGOM AS A WAY OF SAVING THE PLANET

We have covered how lagom is applied in most Swedish homes and how you can use it to change your life. The question lies: How does the lagom lifestyle impacts on a global level? The lagom way might help save our planet by living more modest lives and, therefore, respecting our nature and switching to a more ecological life. The lagom lifestyle suggests you are conscious of your environment and the impact your habits have on it. Just as you strive for doing everything in moderation, take into account how it can moderate impact on the planet and its environment like increasing pollution, damaging ecosystems with littering, or anything else that can harm the planet. In this chapter, we will discover what you can do to lead a better, environmental-friendly life.

The lagom lifestyle is closely connected to conscious habits and buying the things needed and used for functionality instead of impulse buying on a want basis. When we spend our money on things we were taught to believe we should want. We are told by various ads in papers, magazines and on billboards, and TV commercials to want all sorts of different things for ourselves, our homes and our children. But, that can be further from the truth.

Most often, we don't consider the materials or sustainability that are used on the things we buy. This includes items we buy just to sit in the closet or in a drawer that will eventually be thrown out adding to the landfills and trash in the oceans than recycling them. By applying the lagom way in your lives and focusing on building a sustainable life than consumption will bring awareness how money is being spent and why. The Swedish are actually one of the most environmental-friendly countries to live in, and there is much the rest of us can learn from that.

When buying something, anything at all, to consider not only the quality of the things but what materials are used and how it's produced. Pick a material that will last a lifetime and produced in a conscious way. Look for different labels such as eco, cruelty-free or fair trade. There are several different labels like this, and they could vary depending on what country you live in. Read different certificates in your country or state, and what they mean and try to buy things that are produced that way. This will make an impact on the environment, as well as for the people producing them. For example, buying eco coffee means that the people working in the fields work environments are healthier, pay is within the state or country regulations, and so on. Stay conscious of what you buy and how it affects other people. We are all not perfect, including the Swedish, but practice the lagom way often and question why you are buying things, what materials are used, and is it sustainable for long-term usage. For example, watch out for materials in clothes that contain micro-plastics that wash out into the ocean during washing, or switch your ordinary coffee to an ecological brand instead. The taste will be better, that is a promise.

Before buying anything new, determine if you could find the same item at a thrift store or estate sale. Vintage has always been a thing in Sweden and particularly now it is a trend on the rising, where young people buy clothes and furniture from shops, spending time altering the clothes or items to personalize it.

If you do buy new clothes, try to buy brands of good quality that will last throughout time. This is particularly useful for the basics in your wardrobe, like the items used on a daily basis such as shirts, pants, jeans and so on. The Swedish prioritize a classical wardrobe so they can invest in high-quality items than buying multiple cheap items that will have to be replaced each season when they become out of date.

In Sweden, many are moving to the countryside away from the hustle and bustle of the city. Although there are many new homes being built, many choose to buy older homes outside the cities and villages. Many spend their time and money restoring the homes instead of building new homes in these areas, being environmentally-conscious to how new homes can affect the planet. Restoring homes can lead a satisfying effect on your body and mind, and rejuvenate new life into older homes that would have eventually been torn down.

Being environmentally-friendly and conscious, many Swedish have been growing their own plants, vegetables, and fruits in their backyards or balconies. Growing your own food is a huge trend that can save you money. Another added benefit is getting your hands dirty with Mother Nature, which is good for the mind and soul, and provide quality time with yourself and your family. Remember to be lagom and incorporate low maintenance plants like tomatoes, berry bushes, or flowers that require little attention and time. Growing your garden can help improve the quality of air around you, outside and inside your home. There are many benefits incorporating nature in your home and surroundings. While other people are stressed in the cities, making changes in your life can help the planet while finding peace at the same time.

There are, however, many things you can do to live the lagom way and saving the planet that doesn't involve moving or changing your shopping habits. In Sweden, things like plastic reduction, recycling, and zero waste efforts are popular in the lagom lifestyle to living a moderate life, which might include reducing the impact we make on the environment. As a way to minimize this, bring reusable bags to the supermarket, buy sustainable, quality clothes, and minimize your waste. Also, the Swedish people love to recycle almost everything such as plastic, paper, glass bottles, and tin cans and so on, as another way to do what is best for the planet.

CHAPTER 9

21-DAY LAGOM CHALLENGE

We will wrap this book up with twenty-one different challenges to give the Swedish lifestyle a chance and find out if it is a fit for you. Challenge yourself to adopt the lagom lifestyle and have an open mind. Be sure to track your progress in a journal during 21-days to see your progress and what works for you and your family. Some of the challenges will see huge and need more time than just a day to adjust, but choose a small area of your life or home to change and narrow it down little by little. Once you feel confident with a change, continue on with another change until the lagom lifestyle is achieved.

Here's a list to help aid you on your way to achieving the lagom way:

1.Hygge

Instead of attending or hosting a party, meet up with your closest friends and have some hygge time. This might include something simple as a good cup of coffee at a local coffee shop or having a simple dinner at home. The possibilities are endless.

2. Self-care

Schedule some alone time today and do something that recharges your batteries. It could be a walk in the forest or a trail, a bubble bath or staying in bed reading a book for a while in the morning or in the evening. The key is to find tranquility with yourself.

3. Spend time in nature

Get outside and enjoy what's around you. Take a walk, ride your bike or do anything to get you moving. Spending time close to nature is good for your body and soul.

4. Try something new

Why not try a new hobby today. Do something you don't think you'll enjoy doing. You might be surprised. Or, do something that you are afraid of doing skydiving or going to a new town to explore. J If you feel uncomfortable doing it yourself, bring a friend.

5. Take up an old hobby

Rekindle those old hobbies you use to enjoy. Sometimes we quit doing things without even knowing why or when life gets too busy. This will help find peace and tranquility with yourself and your life.

6. Say no

Today's challenge is to say no to something. The Swedish are people pleasers, but they are will say no to things they don't have the time for or feel like doing. Say no to something today, and you'll be surprised at how calm you may feel afterward. Remember, you can't do everything every time for everyone.

7. Settle for good enough

If you are a perfectionist, this will be hard. Sometime today, when you are performing a task, challenge yourself to leave your task once it is done. If you have done it properly, consider it done if it is good enough even if you don't find it perfect. Try it and see what happens. If you don't feel comfortable doing this at work, try at home. When cleaning, settle when it is clean even if there still might be some little thing left to clean. Don't overexert yourself to get things accomplish perfectly each time. No one will probably notice the small imperfection anyway.

8. Declutter your home

Choose a room or small space to start the decluttering process. Do not take on your whole home as it will become overwhelming and discouraging. Tackle a drawer, a cupboard, or closet first, even your desk, to declutter and open up space. Ask yourself questions to assess in the decluttering process:

- Do I use this item on a regular basis?
- Do I need this item (if yes, make sure you know what you need it for)?
- Do I love this item (does it spark joy)?
- Do I need more of this? (Ask this question if you already have multiple similar items).

Only keep the things you use and need. Not all items are useful, some are only decorations and can stay as long as you like the item and as long as it has a given place.

Once you are done, organize what is left and get rid of the clutter through donation or reselling.

9. Declutter and organize your wardrobe

Go through your closet and get rid of the things you no longer use or like. Instead of throwing them out, donate them or sell online. After you have decided what will stay, go ahead and organize your wardrobe, so it is easy to find everything. If this challenge seems too hard becomes overwhelming, narrow it down. Choose one area to begin with like cleaning out your underwear drawer and organize it properly. Then continue on with the rest another day.

10. Choose outfits for a week ahead

Organizing your clothes is one step. Today, plan out your outfits for the week ahead and stick to them. If this seems overwhelming, plan a few days ahead until it becomes a habit you enjoy doing. Planning outfits in advance can save time in the morning and energy. Your clothes are put together already making getting dressed easy and efficient in the morning.

11. Go vintage shopping

Go vintage shopping. Shopping at thrift stores and online helps recycle older clothes and adds personality to your wardrobe and home with unique and one-of-a-kind items. If you don't find the perfect thing, use your imagination and see if you can find something that is easy to alter and incorporate it in your home or wardrobe.

12. Exercise outside

Leave the gym and take your exercise outside. Take in the fresh air and all the benefits of being outdoors. You don't need much equipment or special workout clothes. Lace up your running shoes, comfortable clothes, and go for a brisk walk or run. Feel the need for some strength training? Stop and do pushups and sit-ups, or do them once you get home.

13. Switch sides

If you are usually active and social, try a mindful and calm exercise like yoga or meditation. If you are more of yoga and meditating kind of person, then try an intense and social activity like a spinning class dance class. While mixing up your workouts will help maintain your body, it's a perfect way to find a balance between being social and being in solitude while finding the lagom way in your exercise routine.

14. Plan out meals for one week ahead

Write a meal plan for a week for breakfast, lunch, and dinner and stick to that shopping list and menu. Make the plan according to your taste and circumstances and put it in writing so you will not forget it. If you want more of a challenge, choose dishes with similar ingredients so that you don't have to buy as many items at the grocery store. You can buy less and make sure to use all the food you buy, so you don't have to throw anything away.

15. Write a shopping list and stick to it

Write a shopping list and stick to it at the grocery store. Don't forget to buy other essential items such as toilet paper, detergent and so on. This will help you save time, money, and the energy not to go back to the grocery store multiple times in the week. The more often you go shopping during the week, the more likely you are to impulse buy than need.

16. Swedish cooking

Instead of going out for dinner, try cooking for yourself and eat at home. If you don't have a family who is eating with you, invite a few friends to keep you company. Try a Swedish dish included in this book. If you want to challenge yourself further, make extra food and bring the leftovers to work for lunch the next day and save some money.

17. Pack a snack

Try out a healthy snack instead of coffee and chocolate this afternoon. Prepare a nice and simple snack, like a fruit or a healthy sandwich to eat when you feel those afternoon cravings kicking in.

18. DIY junk food

Gather with your family or friends and cook your own junk food. Make pizza or maybe fries and burgers. The choice is yours. Find a recipe you like and just do it. Eat and enjoy.

19. Recycle your garbage

Gather your trash and recycle it. The Swedish do it all the time. Recycle everything from paper to plastic, and clothes. It is all according to the lagom way, and the Swedish lifestyle where you don't want to leave much damage behind.

20. Educate yourself

The Swedish apply a lagom approach to their shopping habits and how they buy things because they read about products that earth-friendly. So today, read up on environmental-friendly and/or cruelty-free labels. Consider switching over to these brands as they better your options and are sustainable, which is better for the planet.

21. Switch to a friendlier option

Try to use eco, fair trade or cruelty-free products instead of fast and cheaply made items For example, if you are buying new facial products see if you can find an eco-friendly choice or buy ecological fruits the next time you visit the grocery store. Another thing you can do is try to find locally produced products to buy. When buying locally, you are supporting your community. Farmers and small business people will love you for it.

REVIEWS

Reviews and feedback help improve this book and the author. If you enjoy this book, we would greatly appreciate it if you were able to take a few moments to share your opinion and post a review on Amazon.

31036430R00064

Made in the USA
Middletown, DE
27 December 2018